Black and Powerful: The Career Guide for Tomorrow's Top Leaders

By

Ruben Britt, Jr.

© Copyright 2008, Ruben Britt

All Rights Reserved.

No part of this book may be reproduced, stored in a retrieval system, or transmitted by any means, electronic, mechanical, photocopying, recording, or otherwise, without written permission from the author.

ISBN: 978-1-60414-056-9 / 1-60414-056-9

This book is dedicated to my mother, Ida Louis Britt and to my father, the late Ruben Britt, Sr.

"It takes a village to raise a child"

- African Proverb -

Acknowledgements

First and foremost, I would like to thank my Lord and Savior Jesus Christ for whom all blessings flow and for giving me the foresight to write this book. Secondly, I would like to personally thank my loving wife Penny, for her love and support. To my son Ruben III and my daughter Savannah for their love and inspiration. Also, much appreciation to my mentors, Gwendelyn Johnson, the late William Wimberly, Paul Clancy, Wayne Embry and Alfreda Harris for their encouragement and guidance. Finally, to Darrell Ardison for his editing work and for being a true friend for nearly 30 years.

Introduction

From elementary school to college many African-Americans and other minority groups have not been served well by teachers, guidance counselors and career services professionals when it comes to career planning. Aside from this deviant tactic, many of our young brethrens and sisters often lack the life skills that are essential in achieving career success. Like Malcolm X and many other African-Americans, my elementary school teacher tried to coax me into pursuing non-professional careers because she thought that I was good with my hands.

As a career counselor, I am often confronted with situations where young African-Americans and other minority students lack the knowledge and resources for acquiring information related to managing their careers and for finding meaningful employment. *Black and Powerful: The Career Planning Guide for Tomorrow's Leaders* sets forth guidelines that African-Americans and other minority students can follow in choosing and preparing for a career. This book provides a step-by-step process for helping you explore your career aspirations through careful planning and by assessing your abilities, interests and goals. Recognizing that we live in a culture that focuses heavily on technology, careers and culture, African-Americans and other minority students will need to arm themselves with the skills that are imperative for surviving in an age of downsizing, automation and globalization.

The major objectives of the material presented in this book are to help African-Americans and other minority students:

- Understand the importance of education and career planning.
- Assess their abilities, interests, motives, and values, and understand how these personal qualities apply to the skills required in certain occupations.

- Become familiar with the various career and educational resources.
- Understand the importance of gathering information and setting goals/making decisions.
- Plan and implement their decision through education, employment or volunteer training.
- Understand both the job search and interviewing process.

On the other hand, parents are also encouraged to read this book because it can help them understand the career planning process and become familiar with the various resources that are available for helping their children achieve career success.

The ongoing changes in the labor force will require you to learn new skills and remain at the cutting edge with the trends in both the workforce and educational programs. Individuals that become complacent may find themselves expendable or replaced by someone with more skills. Also, many young African-Americans lack management and organizational skills, which are essential in the career planning process.

Career - "Progress or general course of action of a person through life, or through some phase of life, as in some profession or undertaking, some moral or intellectual action. An occupation or profession followed as one's lifework. Success in a profession or occupation."
- The Random House College Dictionary -

Table of Contents

Introduction		vii
Chapter I	The Importance of Career Planning	1
Chapter II	Career Planning and Education – High School	4
Chapter III	A Career Planning Guide for College Students	12
Chapter IV	The Student Athlete: Don't Believe the Hype	17
Chapter V	Studying Tips and Classroom Etiquette	20
Chapter VI	Developing A Portfolio	22
Chapter VII	Resume Writing and Cover Letter	24
Chapter VIII	Interviewing Techniques	40
Chapter IX	Dressing for the Interview	49
Chapter X	Job Search Strategies	51
Chapter XI	Networking	54
Chapter XII	The Career Fair: A Window of Opportunity	56
Chapter XIII	Salary Negotiation	58
Chapter XIV	Professionalism in the Workplace	60
Chapter XV	Preparing for Graduate School	64
Chapter XVI	Financial Aid	67
Chapter XVII	Resources	69
Chapter XVIII	References	71

Chapter I

"To educate a man is to unfit him to be a slave."
- Frederick Douglass -

THE IMPORTANCE OF CAREER PLANNING

Career Planning is a lifelong process that requires careful preparation, commitment and the ability to identify your strengths, weaknesses accompanied by your willingness to acquire new skills. It is a proven fact that the most successful people in the world today are the ones that do more than the average person. This fact holds true in any profession. Whether you are an athlete, a businessperson or entertainer, your success will depend on how much extra time you put into your chosen field.

The success of talk show queen Oprah Winfrey of Harpo Productions and publisher Earl Graves of Black Enterprise are a result of long hours that they spent after five o'clock building their business empires. Also, sports legends Michael Jordan and Jerry Rice attribute their success on the playing field to their off-season conditioning program. Their workout regiment was far more strenuous than the program prescribed to them by their team conditioning coaches. In both examples, the underlying factor to their success was commitment.

It is important to note that the two major factors in career success involves commitment and by making decisions based on your own self-assessment of the direction that you want to take in life. In an ever-changing world, the average person will change their career five to seven times before they retired and get the *gold watch*. The following is a format for developing a career plan:

Self-Assessment

Self-assessment is understanding your personal characteristics such as skills, values, interests and motives. It involves finding answers to the following questions:
- What do I want?
- What am I good at (personal qualities)?
- What are my interests?
- What are my skills?
- What are my strengths?
- What occupations might I like?
- What are my personal values?
- What are my coping styles?
- What motivates me?
- What are my realities and commitment?
- Which subjects do you find interesting or inspiring in school?
- Do you work best alone or in groups?

There are a number of computerized self-assessment tools that may be assessable at your school, local community college or on the Internet. Two of the most commonly used computerized self-assessment programs are Discover and Sigi-Plus. Some of the on-line self-assessment programs are the Keirsey Temperament Sorter (**www.keirsey.com**), the Career Key (**www.sdstest2.com**), the Employment Search Readiness Inventory (**www.careerweb.com/inventory/**) or Black Collegian (**www.blackcollegian.com**).

Getting Information

The next step involves getting information based on the results from your self-assessment query.
- Brainstorm the possibilities (as many as you can think of).
- Narrow down the possibilities.
- Conduct research on your career choice by using the guidance office or the career services center or the library or by talking with others.
- What skills does an occupation require?

- What are the possibilities of advancement in this field?
- What is the potential income in this field?
- What is the employment outlook in this field?
- What are the educational requirements?
- Do I have the skills required for an occupation?

Preparing For A Career
- What kind of training or college education do I need?
- What schools offer this training?
- What kind of tasks do I need to master in the occupation?
- Can I do what is required?
- What is right for me?

Information
- Quite often, many people try to make a career decision without first having the information they need. Therefore, you will need to find out as much as possible about a career before preparing to enter it, or before looking for a job in that field. Obtaining information about a career can be achieved by personal experience, printed materials, on-line or by information interviewing.
- Build a network of contacts.
- If possible, attend career/job fairs and obtain information from employer representatives at the event.

Devising A Game Plan For Your Career
- Making decision (s).
- Setting goals.
- Planning and implementing your decision.
- How do I put my plan into action?

Follow-Up
- Review your decisions and progress.
- Make the necessary adjustments if needed.

Chapter II

"Education is our passport to the future, for tomorrow is for those who prepare for it today".

- Malcolm X -

CAREER PLANNING AND EDUCATION

In 1881, Booker T. Washington urged Blacks to further their education and vocation in order to survive in the post slavery society. That advice still holds true today. We live in a skill-oriented society that is constantly changing. Gone are the days when people could graduate from high school get a job at the local plant or factory, work for 25-30 years and then retire and get the *gold watch*. Today's workers must be armed with the necessary skills that will enable them to survive in an ever-changing world. Those individuals that lack professional or vocational skills will most likely find themselves unemployed or in menial or dead-end jobs. Throughout my travels, I constantly hear some of our young brothers and sisters saying, "I want to get paid." My usual response to that demand is what kind of skills do you have to get paid? The bottom line is, you will need to come to the bargaining table with something more than just being a hard worker. Employers want to know what can you offer to them and what sets you apart from the other candidates.

Recognizing the importance of having a profession, you will need to begin the career planning process as early as your freshman year. You will need to decide if you plan to attend college or vocational school.

Planning To Go To College?

If you are planning to attend college, there are certain steps that you must take to help prepare you for that venture.

Freshman Year
- Develop a list of courses that you plan to take to help prepare you for college. This may require you and your parents to meet with your guidance counselor.
- Develop a list of school and outside activities you plan to participate in. Aside from academic standing, class rank and standardized test scores, college recruiters look for school and community activities.
- Read books, magazines, newspapers or anything that you can get your hands on, because it helps build your vocabulary.
- Get a summer or part-time job and set aside money regularly for your college education.

Sophomore Year

Meet with your guidance counselor and find out what resources are available in the guidance office.

Update plans for college prep courses available to take.

Plan for the PSAT/NMSQT tests in October. <u>Remember, practice makes perfect.</u>

Update your activity list.

Junior Year
- Identify sources of information from guidance counselors, college guidebooks, college fairs or the Internet.
- Register for the PSAT. If you score well on the PSAT, you may be eligible for scholarships and awards.
- Review your high school courses and activity plans.
- Schedule an appointment with your guidance counselor and include your parents.
- Develop a list of career interests.
- List college features that interest you. Example: size of college, location, state/private, cost or diversity.
- Plan to take the SAT I/ACT.

- Familiarize yourself to college costs and discuss it with your parents.
- If you have been successful academically, talk to your guidance counselor about advance level classes.
- Create a preliminary list of the colleges that you are interested in.
- Identify recommendations for college applications.
- Conduct research for financial aid resources.
- Re-enforce your career goals by forming a positive mind set.
- Memorize your social security number. You will need to include it on admission, financial aid and scholarship applications.

Senior Year

Your senior year is the final piece of the puzzle for applying to college. It's during this time period that many students feel overwhelmed. The following steps are monthly activities for helping you through the application process.

September
- It is important that you develop plans to take the SAT I/ACT early.
- Develop a list of two to 10 colleges to which you would like to apply.
- Go to your school library or guidance office and look up the schools of your choice. Ask your guidance counselor for help. Also, you may research this information at your local community college or check the Internet at **www.petersons.com**.
- Locate a SAT/ACT preparatory course/class to help you study for the SAT/ACT. Also, there are a number of computer software materials available that have SAT/ACT preparatory programs that you can purchase at a reasonable price. Make sure that the software programs are approved

by a creditable organization. This information can be found on the cover of the package.
- Talk to your parents or guardians regarding the cost of college, and how much they may be able to contribute.

October
Take the first SAT/ACT that is being offered this month.
Start developing an essay outline for your admission application.
Target the individuals that you plan to ask for recommendations and <u>ask them immediately</u>.
Make plans to visit the colleges of your choice. Find out if they have open house programs or campus tours. There are a number of organizations nationally that sponsor tours for individuals who are interested in attending Historically Black Colleges and Universities (HBCU). You may need to contact the local black professional organizations or community action agencies to obtain this information.
Check sources for financial aid from the library, guidance counselors, private programs, the Internet, and the financial aid office at the local community college.
Start completing financial aid applications promptly. A number of these sources have early deadlines.

November
- Find out what financial aid forms each college requires you to submit (FAFSA; CSS Profile Form).
- It is important to note that early decision applications are expected in the admissions office by November 1–15.
- Begin filling out your early action and rolling admissions applications.
- Make sure that your transcript is returned to your guidance counselor.
- Complete your first draft of your admission application essay.

December
- Complete your admission essay. It should be neat, grammatically correct and interesting. Have someone who is familiar with admission essays proofread it (teacher, guidance counselor).
- Check the deadlines for state and federal government aid programs and obtain the required forms.
- Begin completing the FAFSA form.
- Make sure that you give the guidance office at your high school adequate time to complete the high school report section of the admission application.
- Make sure that all of the college admission applications are neat and accurate. <u>You should read through all applications first before completing them.</u> They are a reflection of you.

January
- Check college application deadlines and make sure that you are on schedule. <u>There is no excuse for being late.</u>
- Send in your FAFSA form, as soon as possible.

February
- Relax and focus on your classes. Try to finish your senior year strong.
- If you were not satisfied with your SAT/ACT scores, you should have made plans to retake the test this month.

March
- If needed, register for the Advance Placement Examinations (A/P). <u>It is important to note that you should only register for the A/P exams only if you think that you can pass them.</u>

April
- A number of colleges announce their admission decisions in April.
- After you have received your acceptance letters, rank your top ten choices.

- Review your financial aid offers and check to see how much of your need is covered.
- If the financial aid package does not meet your need, find out if there are other plans available.

May
- Notify the college of your acceptance <u>immediately</u> after May 1st.
- Contact the Financial Student Aid Information Center (FAFSA: 1-800-433-3242) of your acceptance and have them process your financial aid package as soon as possible.
- If you have not been admitted to any college, <u>contact your guidance counselor immediately.</u>

June
- It is important to note that you should make sure that you accept the financial aid package of the school that you decide to attend.
- Check and find out if you need any additional information to establish and maintain your eligibility for financial aid.
- Exhale, relax and enjoy the summer.

For Non-college Students

If you are not planning to attend college, your career planning goals should continue to be the primary focus. Employers today are looking for someone who is equipped with skills. Therefore, it is imperative that you begin brainstorming on the type of career that you would like to pursue.

Freshman Year
Meet with your guidance counselor and find out what kind of resources are available in the guidance office to help you with planning a career.

If you have decided on a career, find out how you can acquire training in that field. There are a number of high schools throughout the country that offer vocational training and apprenticeship programs.

Sophomore Year
- Read as much information as you can on your career of choice to understand the nature of the field and the kind of job opportunities that may be available after you complete your training.
- Identify your strengths and weaknesses, and focus on improving the areas that you are weak in.

Junior Year
- Create a preliminary list of the schools that you are interested in and make arrangements to visit the schools.
- Research the schools and find out if they are an accredited school by the state or a regional organization. You don't want to end up being scammed by enrolling into one of those *fly-by-night* schools that awards bogus degrees and certifications.
- Talk to students who have graduated from the program.

Senior Year
- Research for resources that can help finance your education. You can check the sources of financial aid from the library, guidance counselors, the Internet, or in the financial aid office at the local community college.
- Start completing financial aid applications promptly. Send in your financial aid form, as soon as possible.

A number of these sources have early deadlines.

January
- Check school application deadlines and make sure that you are on schedule. <u>There is no excuse for being late.</u>

June

- It is important to note that you should make sure that you accept the financial aid package of the school that you decide to attend.
- Check and find out if you need any additional information to establish and maintain your eligibility for financial aid.
- Exhale, relax and enjoy the summer.

Chapter III

Commitment is what transforms a promise into reality.
It is the words that speak boldly of your intentions.
And the actions which speak louder than words.
It is making the time when there is none.
Coming through time after time after time, year after year after year.
Commitment is the stuff character is made of; the power to change the face of things.
It is the daily triumph of integrity over skepticism.
- Anonymous -

A CAREER PLANNING GUIDE FOR COLLEGE STUDENTS

Career planning is a lifelong process that requires careful preparation and the ability to identify your strengths and weaknesses accompanied by your willingness to acquire new skills. It is a proven fact that the most successful people in the world today are the ones that do more than the average person. This fact holds true in any profession. Whether you are an athlete or a businessperson, your success will depend on how much extra time you put into your chosen field.

Your success in the classroom will be determined by how much time you commit yourself to each subject. To state it simple, your effort should not be anything short of a hundred and ten percent (110%).

FRESHMAN - YEAR **EXPLORING THE FRONTIER**
The first year of your college experience must involve exploring the various resources that are available on campus. This wealth of

information will help you make the transition from high school to college smoother.

Learn about the campus resources *(Most importantly, the skills center, tutorial services, the library and computer laboratory)*.

Get to know faculty, counselors, administrators, and other students.

Begin to explore career options by talking to your academic advisor, career counselors and employers *(Career fair)*.

Become aware of your interests, values, and skills through self-assessment, career counseling, or using a career exploration instrument *(Discover, SIGI-PLUS, COPS)*.

Learn and develop new skills through classes, workshops, or on-campus activities.

Take a variety of classes to learn your strengths and interests.

Find out information on who are the best teachers by talking with upper class students, teammates or other athletes.

Develop a portfolio. The creation of a portfolio allows you to collect and record information related to your skills, experience, activities and accomplishments throughout your college experience. It should include the following information:

Resume
Transcript
Letters of references
Evaluations
Thank you letters
Research projects or reports
Certificates
Conferences and workshops attended
Awards
Videotapes
Photographs
Diagrams
Computer discs
Job descriptions from field or past work experiences that are related to your field of interests
Other supporting documents.

SOPHOMORE YEAR - **EYES WIDE OPEN**

The second phase of the career planning process must include arming yourself with information related to careers by studying the academic programs in the college catalogue. Ask yourself, do I know exactly, the requirements to my academic goals? If the answer is no, your work is not done. Visit your academic advisor with your catalog in hand. Also, it is important to acquire a better understanding of yourself by assessing your interests, values, strengths and weaknesses.

Develop a file of information regarding specific career options and narrow your potential career choices.

Examine your own interests and career preferences.

Talk with career services counselors or faculty in the specific field of your choice.

Collect and analyze information on the world of work, professionalism in the workplace and the job outlook for the future.

If possible, take classes in the summer to stay ahead or current with your target graduation date.

If feasible, get a job during the summer months to earn money while you learn new skills, and build a good work reputation and work references.

JUNIOR YEAR - **PREPARING YOUR GAME PLAN**

Now that you have selected a career choice, you should consult with your academic advisor for proper guidance in selecting the appropriate courses in your major.

Conduct an inventory of interests and qualifications that relate to your career goals.

Attend workshops on resume writing and successful interviewing techniques.

Develop a resume and have it professionally critiqued.

Join organizations in your chosen field and attend conferences.

An excellent way for you to gain experience in your chosen field is to participate in an internship. The internship program allows you to acquire new skills and learn about the world of work. It will help increase your chances of employment after graduation.

Expand your network of contacts by talking with career services professionals, employers, faculty members, and by attending career fairs. Research potential employers through various career resource guides and on the Internet in the career services center.

Contact employers that hire people in your field of concentration and schedule information interviews.

SENIOR YEAR - **PUTTING YOUR GAME PLAN INTO ACTION**

At the beginning of your senior year, you must kick start your job search campaign into high gear. Commit yourself to a thorough search. The job search process is very similar to sports. If you expect to be successful, you must know the rules, develop a sound game plan and put in the time to execute it.

Assess your experience, abilities, accomplishments, and skills and evaluate where your talents can be best used *(Review your portfolio)*.

Attend on-campus workshops that address such topics as interviewing techniques, resume writing and job search strategies. If possible, you should participate in a mock interview.

Discuss career opportunities with career counselors, faculty, friends, associates and network contacts. Seventy-percent (70%) of the jobs in the U.S. are obtained through the network system.

Schedule interviews on-campus and on-site with as many employers as possible.

Attend job fairs and research potential employers through the use of the career services library. Utilize the various career development publications in the career center to identify companies and organizations that are actively recruiting job candidates.

Develop a system for keeping track of the number of employers whom you sent your resume to *(Use index cards, or a notebook or create a database on the computer)*.

When sending out a resume, you should submit a well-written cover letter and resume in a 9" x 12" envelope. Before you send out your cover letter and resume, make sure that you have a professional critique them.

Conduct follow-up telephone calls to employers a week after you have sent out your cover letter and resume.

Do not get discouraged if you receive rejection letters. It is all part of the process of finding a job.

Chapter IV

"The will to win, the desire to succeed, the urge to reach your full potential - these are the keys that will unlock the door to personal excellence."

- Coach Eddie Robinson -

THE STUDENT ATHLETE: DON'T BELIEVE THE HYPE

All too often, a number of student athletes tend to disregard the importance of education and they generally devote all of their energies to sports. To put it simple, they drop the word student from student athlete and they view themselves as athletes. This unconcerned attitude towards academics is ingrained in their minds early in their lives for a number reasons including their coaches, their parent's failure to emphasize the importance of education and by their schools willingness to win at any cost. Many of our misguided student athletes tend to overlook academics and set their sights on becoming a professional athlete. Oblivious to the fact that only a small percentage (1.9%) of athletes make it to the big leagues, a number of our young black athletes are willing to sidestep their education for a long shot in the limelight.

One of the many tragedies in sports is seeing a number of athletes displaying their ignorance during an interview on television. Their inability to articulate their performance with the use of proper grammar in front of a camera depicts their lack of education and it gives credence to the term *dumb jock*. Many of these uneducated athletes limit their opportunities outside of their sport and they generally end up running into a dead end after their playing days are over. More important, as an athlete, you are always one step away from a career ending injury. Therefore, it is imperative that you always have a backup plan that is career and education related.

Another factor that deters student athletes from committing themselves to the classroom is the distractions from recruiters and scouts. Quite often, recruiters and scouts tend to disregard the importance of academics by requesting to meet with athletes during class hours. Also, they sometimes put undue pressure on a student by demanding that the student athlete meet with them during school hours because they are heavily booked with appointments. As a result of these ill-advised meetings, the student ends up falling behind in class, which can sometimes results into failure. If a recruiter or scout is truly concerned about your well-being, then they should be considerate enough to schedule a meeting with you after class or at a time that is convenient for you. This newfound hype and celebrity status from being an athlete can often cause you to discard your attention in the classroom. It is important to note <u>that you are a student first and an athlete second</u>.

Your success in the classroom will be determined by how much time you commit yourself to each subject. You should approach each class in the same manner that you do on the playing field. Balancing academics and athletics will require you to manage your time effectively, utilize the resources around you and by having a burning desire to complete your high school or college degree. To state it simple, your effort should not be anything short of a hundred and ten percent (110%).

<u>Questions to Ask the Coach/Recruiter</u>

1. What does the scholarship consist of? (Room, board, books, tuition)
2. How many degree programs does your institution offer?
3. Are all of your degree programs accredited?
4. What is the graduation rate of your athletes?
5. What kinds of student support services programs are available for your athletes?
6. Do you provide assistance or resources for summer school?

7. What kind of off-season conditioning program do you provide for your athletes?
8. How many players have you recruited for the position that I would be playing?
9. Does your college have a support program for athletes who want to complete their degree after their eligibility is up?
10. What kind of defense or offense do you employ?

Chapter V

"With education, the tongue becomes mightier than the sword."
- Anonymous -

STUDYING TIPS AND CLASSROOM ETIQUETTE

Studying Tips
Your success in the classroom will be determined by your study methods and by how you manage your time effectively.

Choose a place where you are least likely to be distracted.
Schedule your study time in a place where you're less likely to see friends or teammates (library, skills center or study hall).
Study in a position that is comfortable and non-conducive to sleeping.
Study during the time that you have scheduled and ***do not*** stray way from the your game plan.
Maintain concentration and pursue the material with a positive approach.
If needed, modify your studying techniques to help you memorize the material. This may require you to review the material again or quiz yourself periodically or by writing the material out on paper.
Apply the study material to real life situations.

Classroom Etiquette
Sit towards the front of the classroom. It helps you stay focused on what is being discussed in class.
Take good notes and write a summary of each class. It will help you remember the topic that was presented in class.
Get to know your instructors. This may require you to meet with them after class or during their office hours.
Study in advance the material that will be discussed in the next class and write notes or draw diagrams. This will make it easier for you

to better understand the material being presented and it will allow you to stay ahead in class.

The best way to earn a **failing grade** is by **not attending class**. Your attendance in class will play a major role in your success as a student.

Chapter VI

"Knowledge is like a garden: if it is not cultivated, it cannot be harvested."

- African Proverb -

DEVELOPING A PORTFOLIO

Successful interviewing requires strategic planning and knowing how to market yourself effectively to employers. During the pre-interview stage it's important to prepare for all phases of the interview. By anticipating what lies ahead and by knowing how to communicate your strengths and accomplishments to a perspective employer. However, it is imperative that you are able to identify and assess your strengths before the interview takes place. This is done by conducting a complete self-assessment of yourself. Self-assessment requires identifying specific skills, accomplishments, work experiences and other non-work related experiences that will allow you to emphasize specific competencies. Once you make this assessment, the ideal strategy for packaging those skills for presentation to an employer is through the portfolio. The portfolio is designed to allow you to highlight evidence of your skills, accomplishments and capabilities to perspective employers. It encourages self-evaluation, self-acknowledge and it provides a developmental look at your progress.

Today, many college students are involved in activities outside of the classroom related to roles in both their personal and professional development. The creation of a portfolio allows you to document significant activities that took place during your college experience. You should begin developing a portfolio during your freshmen year. However, other experiences, including work, community involvement and appropriate volunteer experience prior to the college experience should be documented.

What goes in a portfolio?
A portfolio should consist of the following:
- Resume
- Job descriptions from field experiences or past work experiences that are related to your field of interests
- Letters of references
- Evaluations
- Transcripts
- Thank you letters
- Awards and citations
- Research projects or reports
- Certificates or certifications
- Articles or work samples
- Conferences and workshops attended
- Videotapes, DVDs, photographs, diagrams or computer disc
- Presentation notes, outlines or other supporting documentation

Traditionally, portfolios were generally used by art, communication and theater majors as a vehicle for showcasing their work in an interview. The highly visual nature of a portfolio makes it the ideal vehicle for students majoring in other disciplines to support their accomplishments by actual demonstration of skills and contributions. The existence of a portfolio will help to develop confidence in your abilities and better prepare you for the interviewing process.

Chapter VII

"Our legacy is to persevere and overcome. To do otherwise is not an option."

- Earl Graves -

RESUME WRITING AND COVER LETTER

THE PURPOSE OF A RESUME
The resume is your official representative that reflects your best qualities, experiences, educational training and achievements. It is a verbal portrait designed to help you obtain an interview.

There are three types of resumes.
Reverse Chronological
Functional
Combination

It is important for you to determine which style of resume fits best for you?

REVERSE CHRONOLOGICAL RESUME
The reverse chronological resume is formatted to read from most recent to least recent in education and work. It is utilized when there is a void or gaps in employment or education. It is the easiest form to write.

<u>*Example:*</u> **The Reverse Chronological Resume**

PROFESSIONAL EXPERIENCE
Editorial Assistant   December 1998 - present
Tupac Publications   Def Jam, MN
Currently serving as series editor for books on rap music.
Developed and copyedited a book on health and nutrition, working with author, publisher and illustrator to organize and refine manuscript.

Assist in monitoring interns.

FUNCTIONAL RESUME
Is used when there are lapses in dates of employment or education.
Is used when individuals are in transition.
Is used when individuals are seasoned professionals.
Highlights skills as opposed to title.
When the resume is more than one page.

Example: **Functional Resume**

PROFESSIONAL EXPERIENCE
Management
- Managed gift shop and supervised employees.
- Planned and directed meetings.

Production and Design
- Conducted inventory and processed invoices.

COMBINATION RESUME
The combination resumes affords you the opportunity to utilize your creativity to build a style that takes into account the best parts of the reverse chronological and functional.

The Heading
The heading should include:
Your full name with middle initial
Address
Telephone number
E-mail (Refrain from using outlandish email addresses i.e. hipcity@coldmail.com)

Example: **Heading**

**ROSE ROYCE
123 Wantajob Lane
Anywhere, NJ 12345
(856)987-6543
E-mail: rroyce@resume**
(Font should be in bold)

The Objective
Gives the reader a clear indication as to the position being sought and it gives the resume direction. It should be clear and to the point.

Example: Objective
- Seeking an entry-level position in management utilizing strong organizational and leadership skills.
- Seeking an entry-level position in accounting utilizing my analytical and computer skills.

Summary of Qualifications
The summary of qualifications is your marketing pitch, which allows you to boast about your talents. It should correspond with your objective and it should include specific achievements, certifications, licenses, computer skills, or other job-related skills. It is important that you list only the skills and achievements that will help you with the position that you are seeking.

Example: Summary of Qualifications
- Excellent organizational and communication skills.
- Computer literate; experience includes word processing, spreadsheets, and database management.
- Fluent in French and Spanish.
- Successfully published photographs in national and regional magazines.

Education
The name of your college / university or trade school, the city and state.

Degree granted and the month and year it was received or expected graduation date.

If you have attended more than one college, list them in chronological order starting with your most recent college and include dates attended or the degree/certificate received.

Example: **Education**
Sojourner University   Ipswich, MA
Bachelor of Arts in Communication   May 2000
Dean's List   GPA 3.45 (Include GPA if it is 3.0 or higher)

Bayside Community College   Zackery, LA
Associate of Science in Liberal Arts   May 1998

Related Courses:
Photojournalism, Publications Layout and Design, Journalistic Writing, News Reporting

Work Experience
When listing your work experience, choose the title that best fits you.

Example: **Work Experience**
                    Employment History
Related Experience
                    Professional Experience

List places of employment chronologically starting with your present or your most recent job.

Give the name of the organization, city and state, dates that you worked (month / year), your job title, and a brief description of your duties.

Use action words to describe job responsibilities (See page 30). Be direct and concise.

Each line should be read in the first person, with the pronouns I, my, or we omitted.

Current positions should be written in the present tense; past positions should be written in the past tense.

Example:
- Developed and implemented student leadership program.

(End each statement with a period.)

Should you have more than one version of your resume?
Yes! When applying for different jobs which require different skills.

Resume Checklist
Information fits neatly on one page.
Name, address, telephone number & e-mail address are on the top of paper.
Margins should be a standard inch on all four sides of paper.
Print and layout should be reader friendly!
Font size 10 -14 points.
Have someone professional who is familiar with resumes critique it.
NO ERRORS!

BUILD A RESUME

Name: _____

Home Address: _____   College Address: _____

Street: _____   Street: _____

City: _____ State: ____ Zip: _____   City: _____ State: ____ Zip: ____

Phone: _____   Phone: _____

Email: _____

Job Objective (Indicate your work direction; be as specific as possible.)
_____
_____

Education
Name of College: _____ *City:* _____ *State:* _____
Degree: _____ *Expected Graduation Date:* _____
GPA: _____ (If 3.0 or higher)

Course Highlights: (Use primarily in resumes for internships.)
_____
_____

Work Experience (Start with most recent place of employment.)
Job Title: _____ *Period Employed:* _____
Name of Company, City, State _____
Responsibilities: (Use action words.) _____
_____

Skills:
_____
_____

Awards:
_____
_____

Activities & Interests:
_____
_____

References available upon request.

Resume Action Words

abstract (ed)	budget (ed)	describe (d)	forecast (ed)
accelerate (d)	calculate (d)	design (ed)	formulate (d)
accomplish (ed)	capture (d)	determine (d)	found (ed)
account (ed)	catalogue (d)	develop (ed)	furnish (ed)
achieve (d)	categorize (d)	devise (d)	generate (d)
act (ed)	challenge (d)	diagram (ed)	govern (ed)
activate (d)	change (d)	discover (ed)	handle (d)
adapt (ed)	choreograph (ed)	direct (ed)	help (ed)
add (ed)	clarify (ied)	discern (ed)	hire (d)
administer (ed)	classify (ied)	display (ed)	illustrate (d)
advance (d)	coach (ed)	distribute (d)	illuminate (d)
advertise (d)	compare (d)	draw (drew)	implement (ed)
advise (d)	compile (d)	earn (ed)	import (ed)
aid (ed)	complete (d)	educate (d)	improve (d)
align (ed)	compose (d)	eliminate (d)	increase (d)
allocate (ed)	comprehend (ed)	employ (ed)	infer (red)
amuse (d)	compute (d)	encourage (d)	influence (d)
analyze (d)	conceive (d)	engineer (ed)	inform (ed)
answer (ed)	conceptualize (d)	enhance (d)	initiate (d)
anticipate (d)	condense (d)	enlarge (d)	innovate (d)
appoint (ed)	conduct (ed)	enrich (ed)	inquire (d)
approve (d)	construct (ed)	establish (ed)	inspect (ed)
arbitrate (d)	consult (ed)	entertain (ed)	install (ed)
arrange (ed)	contract (ed)	evaluate (d)	institute (d)
assemble (d)	control (ed)	examine (d)	instruct (ed)
assess (ed)	convince (d)	exchange (d)	interpret (ed)
assist (ed)	cooperate (d)	execute (d)	interrogate (d)
assume (d)	coordinate (d)	expand (ed)	interview (ed)
augment (ed)	counsel (ed)	expedite (d)	introduce (d)
awaken (ed)	craft (ed)	experience (d)	intuit
award (ed)	create (d)	explore (d)	invent (ed)
began	critique (d)	extend (ed)	inventory
boost (ed)	dance (d)	facilitate (d)	investigate (d)
broaden (ed)	define (d)	fluency	judge (d)
build (built)	delegate (d)	focus (ed)	launch (ed)
buy (bought)	demonstrate (d)	follow (ed)	layout

learn (ed)
lecture (d)
liaison
link (ed)
list (ed)
maintain (ed)
manage (d)
market (ed)
mediate (d)
merge (d)
modify (ied)
model (ed)
monitor (ed)
motivate (d)
negotiate (d)
observe (d)
organize (d)
orient (ed)
originate (d)
participate (d)
perform (ed)
persuade (d)
plan (ned)
play (ed)
prepare (d)
present (ed)
preside (d)
probe (d)

problem solve
process (ed)
produce (d)
proficiency
profit (ed)
program (med)
progress (ed)
project (ed)
propose (d)
promote (d)
prove (d)
provide (d)
publicize (d)
purchase (d)
quantify (ied)
qualify (ied)
question (ed)
read
received
recommend (ed)
reconstruct (ed)
record (ed)
recruit (ed)
redefine (d)
reduce (d)
refer (ed)
regulate (d)
reinforce (d)

reorganize (d)
render (ed)
represent (ed)
request (ed)
require (d)
research (ed)
respond (ed)
responsible
restructure (d)
revamp (ed)
review (ed)
revise (d)
rewrite
screen (ed)
schedule (d)
seek (sought)
select (ed)
set up
sing (sang)
sketch (ed)
solve (d)
stimulate (d)
streamline (d)
strengthen (ed)
structure (d)
style (d)
substitute (d)
suggest (ed)

supervise (d)
support (ed)
survey (ed)
strategize (d)
synthesize (d)
systematize (d)
teach (taught)
tend (ed)
test (ed)
trade (d)
train (ed)
transform (ed)
translate (d)
troubleshoot (ed)
tutor (ed)
understand
understood
unify (unified)
unite (d)
update (d)
upgrade (d)
use (d)
utilize (d)
valuate (d)
vend (ed)
verify (ied)
volunteer (ed)
write (wrote)
work (ed)

Ruben Britt, Jr.

Sample of a Chronological Resume

ROSE ROYCE
123 Main Road
Anywhere, MA 01234
617.987.XXXX
chronological.resume@cap

JOB OBJECTIVE

An entry-level accounting position with potential for advancement.

SUMMARY OF QUALIFICATIONS

- Computer literate, experience includes Word 6.0, Excel and database management.
- Excellent organizational and communication skills.
- Fluent in Japanese and Spanish.
- Certified in sign language.

EDUCATION

MATTAPAN UNIVERSITY	Milton, MA
Bachelor of Science, Accounting	May 2002

- Dean's List - GPA 3.45
- Completed independent study in International Business

SUFFOLK COUNTY COLLEGE	Dorchester, MA
Associate of Arts and Science, Business Studies	May 2000

Related Courses:
Managerial Accounting, Auditing, Cost Accounting, Advanced Accounting, and Individual Taxation

RELATED PROFESSIONAL EXPERIENCE

TEACHING ASSISTANT	August 2000 to Present
Roxbury County College	Roxbury, MA

- Assist professor with Urban Enterprise Zone research project.
- Tutor students, maintain class records, and correct papers.

BOOKKEEPER Summer 1999
Franklin Museum Mission Hill, MA
- Verified and entered details of financial transactions into computer system.
- Balanced books and compiled statistical reports.
- Calculated general ledger and employee wages.

ADDITIONAL EXPERIENCE
SALESPERSON Summer 1997, 1998
Grove Hall Fashions Roxbury, MA
- Performed sales duties while coordinating store displays and floor moves.

REFERENCES
Available Upon Request

Sample of a Functional Resume

NATHAN TURNER
21 Jump Street
Waterproof, LA 20034
504.504.5040
nat.turner@bol.com

JOB OBJECTIVE
Seeking an entry-level position in pubic relations utilizing strong organizational and communication skills.

SUMMARY OF QUALIFICATIONS
- Completed an intensive six-month internship program in public relations with the State Department.
- Demonstrated success in creating public service announcements and webpage design.
- Possess strong organization and communication skills.
- Highly motivated and committed to professional excellence.

- Computer literate in Microsoft Office, Power Point, Harvard Graphics and webpage design.

PROFESSIONAL EXPERIENCE
Communications and Public Relations
Created brochures, public service announcements and promotional packages.
Designed webpage, office logo and layout for newsletter.
Conducted presentations and attended press conferences.
Communicated effectively with the media, community leaders, education constituents and other professionals.

Administration
Trained new employees and devised monthly reports.
Implemented a new database system and developed an instruction manual.
Coordinated recycling program and assisted in special projects.

EMPLOYMENT HISTORY
2002 – 2003 **Intern** U.S. State Department – Washington, DC
2000 – 2002 **Assistant Manager** The Stax Foundation – Monroe, LA
1999 – 2000 **Cashier** Spin City Markets – East Cupcake, LA

EDUCATION
Southern Louisiana College Baton Rouge, LA
B.S. in Communication, May 2003
Specialization: Public Relations

References available upon request.

Sample of a Combination Resume

GOMEZ ADDAMS
21 Jump Street
East Cupcake, NJ 08034
856.504.5040
goaddams@bol.com

JOB OBJECTIVE
Seeking an entry-level position in pubic relations utilizing strong organizational and communication skills.

EDUCATION
Rowdy University Glassboro, NJ
B.S. in Communication, May 2003
Specialization: Public Relations

COURSE HIGHLIGHTS
Introduction to Public Relations, Media Planning, Publication Layout & Design, Print Media Copywriting, Advanced Public Relations Writing, Marketing Basics

SUMMARY OF QUALIFICATIONS
    Completed an intensive six-month internship program in public relations with the State Department.
    Demonstrated success in creating public service announcements and webpage design.
    Possess strong organization and communication skills.
    Highly motivated and committed to professional excellence.

PROFESSIONAL EXPERIENCE
Communications and Public Relations
    Created brochures, public service announcements and promotional packages.
    Designed webpage, office logo and layout for newsletter.
    Conducted presentations and attended press conferences.
    Communicated effectively with community leaders, education constituents and other professionals.

Administration
    Trained new employees and devised monthly reports.

Implemented a new database system and developed an instruction manual.
Coordinated recycling program and assisted in special projects.

COMPUTER SKILLS
Microsoft Office, Power Point, Harvard Graphics and webpage design.

EMPLOYMENT HISTORY
2002 – 2003 **Intern** U.S. State Department – Washington, DC
2000 – 2002 **Assistant Manager** The Stax Foundation – Millville, NJ
1999 – 2000 **Cashier** Spin City Markets – East Cupcake, NJ

References available upon request.

COVER LETTER

YOUR PRESENT ADDRESS
CITY, STATE
ZIP CODE

Date of Correspondence

Name of Individual
Title
Name of company/organization
Address
City, State, Zip Code

Dear Mr./Mrs./Ms. (Last Name):

PARAGRAPH ONE
Tell why you are writing. Name the position, field or general area in which you are interested. Tell how you found out about the position.

PARAGRAPH TWO
Describe your professional/educational qualifications. Cite one or two areas of qualification experience, which specifically qualify you for

the position. Emphasize particular areas of related experience and training. Stress why you are unique, special and the perfect person for the position.

PARAGRAPH THREE
Close by noting that you have enclosed a copy of your resume and that you will provide any additional information requested. Note that you will look forward to a future response and that you would like to schedule an interview. Include your telephone number.

Sincerely,

Name

Sample of Cover Letter

Don Serious
617 Redwood Drive
Visalia, CA 98028
(209) 256-4322

May 12, 2002

Ms. Jasmine Thomas
Human Resources Manager
Shaniqua Pharmaceuticals
856 Golden Gate Parkway
Hanford, CA 98028

Dear Ms. Thomas:

In response to the advertisement in the Lakewood Examiner for the position of salesperson for Shaniqua Pharmaceuticals, I hereby submit my letter of application.

In my career, I have experience in sales with Tulare Medical Supply servicing customers who enter our store. Through reading professional periodicals and magazines that are sent to me as an employee of Tulare Medical Supply, I have become very knowledgeable of the different types of medical supplies. This knowledge enables me to fully service our customers' medical supply needs and address all of their questions. Of particular interest to you, I increased sales this year by 20% over last year's figures. In light of my accomplishment, my supervisor has given me the responsibility of developing a plan to market medical supplies to local drug stores. In addition to my work experience, I recently completed a course in drug/pharmacology terminology at the University of California in Fresno. Upon completion of this course, I increased my knowledge of medicines and their effects.

In closing, I have always had a strong interest in the medical/pharmaceutical sales field and have attempted to gain experience and the knowledge to work effectively in that capacity. With that in mind, I feel I am the best candidate for the position of salesperson for Shaniqua Pharmaceuticals. Enclosed you will find my resume. I can be reached at (209) 256-4332 or on my cell phone at (209) 222-2348.

Thank you for your time and consideration.

Respectfully,

Don Serious

Sample of Cover Letter

Jay Byrd
321 Orchard Park
Birmingham, AL 25029
(205) 863-9547

April 10, 2003

Mr. Marshall Law
Personnel Director
Crabtree & Law
1234 Copley Place
Worcester, AL 20555

Dear Mr. Law,

Anticipating graduation in May 2004, I would like to take this opportunity to express interest in a management trainee position with Crabtree and Law.

As an honor student, at Rockwell College, I was chosen to intern for the local consulting firm of Quicksand and Associates. At Quicksand and Associates, I was responsible for upgrading the reporting procedures and their database system. My supervisor, Mr. Jimmy Slack, was so impressed with my knowledge and performance that he invited me to continue my internship for another semester. Furthermore, the experience afforded me the opportunity to learn the importance of maintaining customer relations and having strong organizational skills in a business environment. I feel that my past work experience and my educational training has prepared me to understand the rudiments of the position as management trainee.

Enclosed is a copy of my resume, which outlines in detail my credentials. Given the opportunity, I look forward to meeting you for a personal interview to discuss my qualifications. I will be calling you the week of April 29th to arrange a convenient time. I can be reached at (856) 863 – 9547.

Thank you for your consideration.

Sincerely,

Jay Byrd

Chapter VIII

"If you have no confidence in self, you are twice defeated in the race of life. With confidence, you have won even before you have started."

- Marcus Garvey -

INTERVIEWING TECHNIQUES

Successful interviewing requires careful planning, which involves a number of basic steps for helping you secure a job. Failure to incorporate a solid game plan in your job search will decrease your chances of a landing a job or cause you to bomb out in an interview.

Types of interviews

- <u>One on One</u> – The one on one interview can sometimes evolve into a group interview.
- <u>Group</u> – The group interview is a situation where several people ask the candidate questions.
- <u>Telephone</u> – You should approach the telephone interview in the manner as the one on one interview. Make sure that you are in a comfortable room with no distractions. Allow yourself enough time to relax before the interview.
- <u>Luncheon or Dinner</u> – This is a situation where your table etiquette comes into focus. All the things that your parents told you about eating at the table *(Don't talk with your mouth full of food. Take small bites.).* Do not order the most expensive food on the menu and refrain from alcohol beverages. If you have a choice between soup and salad, order the soup. Soup is easier to eat. Don't order desert unless the interviewer orders it. You don't want to keep them waiting. They may need to get back to the office. Always thank them for the lunch or dinner.

Preparing for the interview
1. Conduct an honest assessment of yourself and focus on your skills, talents and aspirations. *How do your skills add to the job that you are seeking?*
2. Assess your strengths and weaknesses. *What are your strengths?* (Skills, educational training or work experience) *What are your weaknesses?* (Assess weaknesses and devise a solution for improvement) Make a list of your weaknesses and specify what you are doing to improve them.
3. Research the position that you are interviewing to determine what the responsibilities are. You should be able to find this information on the employer's annual report materials or their Webpage. If you have difficulty finding information on the position, you should research the information in the Dictionary of Occupational Titles (DOT). The DOT is a publication that is produced by the U.S. Department of Labor, which provides an updated description of occupations.
4. Identify which skills are applicable to the job that you are seeking. Important note, being a hard worker does not count as a skill.
5. Research the employer and understand the salary expectations and industry reviews - Prior to your interview, you should be able to answer the following questions regarding the organization.
    a.) What is the complete name and address of the organization?
    b.) What type of activity is the organization involved in?
    c.) What are the primary products and services of this organization?
    d.) What is the size of the organization? (Large, medium, or small organization)
    e.) What is the total number of employers working in the organization?
    f.) What is the total amount of annual sales or income of the organization?
    g.) Is the employer a private, state, or federal organization?
    h.) Does the organization have facilities in other locations?
    i.) What is the growth potential of the organization?

j.) What other information about the organization do you think might be of value to you in the interview?
6. You should have a clear understanding of the interview process. *What is expected of you?*
7. The interview process involves role-playing and having a polished appearance. *Do you look the part?* Looking the part consists of having a professional look, which includes hair design, facial appearance and the type of clothes that you wear. *You can't expect a professional salary, if you don't have a professional image.* Image is a key element in successful interviewing and it often separates the top candidate from the rest of the pool. You should present a professional image that depicts you as a part of the organization. *(See Chapter on Dress for Success)*
8. <u>Turn off your cell phone, beeper or any other electronic devices</u>.
9. There are several interviewing stages that must be completed during the day of the interview.
   a.) Arrive 15 – 20 minutes early
   b.) Bring an ink pen along with two extra copies of your resume.
   c.) Speak to everyone that you come in contact with including the clerical staff *(receptionist/secretary)* or security guard.
   d.) Listen and prepare thoughts before speaking.
   e.) Speak clearly and refrain from using slang or other negative verbal gestures *(ah, uhms, you know, ah hum, etc.)* Avoid tentative, indecisive terms such as *"I feel"*, *"I guess"*, *and "I think."* Make sure that your answers are clear and concise. You don't want to turn the interviewer off by giving long answers.
   f.) <u>Never discuss salary/money</u> before they offer you the job. Focus on the job responsibilities and what you have to offer them.
   g.) Get the names of all the interviewers or persons that you come in contact with. If possible, try to get their business cards.
   h.) Greet the contact person by their last name (Mr. ___ or Ms.___) with a firm handshake (two humps).

i.) Throughout the interview maintain eye contact.
j.) Wait until you are instructed to have a seat.
k.) Sit up straight in your chair and lean slightly forward. Leaning forward in your seat can look intimidating and leaning back in your chair can look too relaxed. Keep your feet on the floor and avoid crossing your legs. Also, keep your arms by your side on the armrest of the chair.
l.) If you are offered coffee, tea, soda or juice, <u>decline</u>. You need to focus on the task at hand, which is interviewing and not be straddled with eating distractions.
m.) Avoid any nervous gestures that you might have such as tapping your feet, playing with your hair or biting your fingernails.
n.) Nonverbal communication is extremely important in an interview. It consists of the following:

- appropriate dress
- proper grooming
- appropriate handshake
- maintaining posture
- listening
- sitting appropriately in a chair
- entering or leaving a room
- facial expression
- the movement of your head
- use of hands
- eye contact
- eating
- greeting others
- drinking

o.) Avoid wearing perfume, cologne, strong smelling hair sprays or grease.
p.) Personal hygiene is also important, therefore you should check yourself for bad breath or body order. *(You don't want to turn the interviewer off with poor hygiene.)*
q.) Remove all body piercing items from your body.
r.) Wear natural hair color *(Avoid roots)*.
s.) Ladies – Wear minimal makeup that portrays a natural look.
t.) Ladies – Wear stud or small loop earrings.
u.) Fingernails must be well manicured.
v.) Men – Remove earrings.
w.) Minimal jewelry.

If possible, you may want to schedule a mock interview with your career services center or with someone who has experience in conducting interviews. Finally, it is important that you portray a positive demeanor by smiling. *(Simply project a look of enthusiasm, confidence and don't try to show all 32 teeth.)*

Sample Interview Questions

Tell me about yourself. (Do not discuss personal information. Tell them why you are the ideal person for the position)
Why should we hire you?
What are your strengths?
What are your weaknesses?
Why did you choose to interview with our company?
Why do you want to work for our organization?
Where do you see yourself in five years?
Give me three adjectives that describe you as a person?
What new skills have you developed in the past year?
What do you know about our company?
Why did you choose your major?
How do you work under pressure? Give an example.
What extra-curricular activities did you participate in while in school?
Are you capable of working on multiple assignments at once?
What are your career goals?
How do you feel about working overtime?
What can you offer us?
What was the most difficult aspect of your last job?
How would your former supervisor describe your work performance?
What two or three accomplishments have given you the most satisfaction?
What did you enjoy most about your last job?
What did you least enjoy about your last job?
Do you prefer working individually or working in groups?
What motivates you in a job?

Questions one, two and three are interrelated because they require answers that reflect your skills, capabilities and educational training. Take advantage of this opportunity and demonstrate to the interviewer why you are the ideal person for the position. Before the interview, you should review these questions and determine how you will respond to them. Also, review your resume, portfolio or any other materials that demonstrates your skills and related experience.

Questions to ask the employer

Although you may feel that you are in the hot seat during the interview, it is important to understand that you are interviewing the employer. You need to know if this company or organization is the right fit for you. Interviewers expect job candidates to ask them pertinent questions during the interview. Therefore, you should develop a list of questions to ask them when opportunity permits. The following is a sample list of questions to ask during interview.

1. What are the company's plans for future growth?
2. What are the challenging aspects of the job?
3. What kind of benefits does your company offer? (health, dental, eye care, etc.)
4. Does your company provide orientation for new employees?
5. Does your company offer tuition reimbursement for its employees?
6. What skills are especially important for someone in this position?
7. Is this a new position or am I replacing someone?
8. What are the company's plans for future growth?
9. How has this company fared during the recent recession?
10. How is an employee evaluated and promoted?
11. Why should I want to work for this organization?
12. Why do you enjoy working for this company?
13. What kind of qualities are you looking for in your new hires?
14. Describe the work environment?
15. What are the opportunities for personal growth?
16. What is the typical career path for a person in this position?
17. What makes this company different from its competitors?
18. Is it company policy to promote within?

19. When do you expect to make a decision regarding this position?

More importantly, <u>do not ask about the salary</u> unless they offer you the position.

At the conclusion of the interview, ask the interviewer for their business card. After the interview, take notes on what occurred during the interview and send the interviewer a thank you letter. The thank you letter allows you to thank them for taking the time to meet with you and to reaffirm that you are still interested in the position. Also, it allows you to hammer home key points about your background that you failed to mention in the interview.

Sample – Thank You Letter Format

Your address
City, State, Zip
Telephone number

Date of correspondence

Name of interviewer
Job title
Name of company/organization
Address
City, State, Zip

Dear Mr./Ms./Mrs. (Last name):

<u>Paragraph One</u> - Indicate that you enjoyed meeting with him or her to discuss employment opportunities at (name of company/organization).

Paragraph Two – Reaffirm your interest in working for this particular company/organization and reiterate why you are the ideal person for this position.

Paragraph Three – In closing, indicate that you look forward to hearing from them soon, or by the date that they discussed with you in the interview.

Sincerely,

Your name

Sample – Thank You Letter

21 Jump Street
East Cupcake, MT xxxxx
(123)555-xxxxx

Date

Mr. Marshall Law
Recruiter
XYZ Company
1776 Sesame Street
West Cupcake, MT xxxxx

Dear Mr. Law:

Thank you for taking the time to meet with me yesterday to discuss the management position with XYZ Company. The information you provided me with was very beneficial.

Ruben Britt, Jr.

As we discussed, the experience I gained from working as a part-time assistant manager at ABC Textiles will be directly applicable to the position your company has available in its Human Resources Department.

In closing, I would like you to know that I am very interested in joining the XYZ Company as a Management Trainee and I look forward to hearing from you in the near future to discuss my qualifications further.

Sincerely,

Rose Royce

Chapter IX

"Over every mountain there is a path, although it may not be seen from the valley."
- James Rogers -

DRESSING FOR THE INTERVIEW

Men
- Wear business types suit; Recommended colors: navy blue, black, dark gray or brown. Refrain from wearing corduroy, denim, plaids, suede or leather.
- Wear a long-sleeved white shirt. (Neutral colored collared shirt) Do not wear a silk or shining texture shirt.
- Single-breasted suits should not exceed four buttons. Always leave the bottom button unbutton.
- Socks should match your suit pants or your shoes.
- Wear a conservative tie that matches your suit. Avoid wearing bow ties, clip-on ties or ties with pictures on them.
- Shoes should be shined and well preserved. It is highly recommended that you purchase a pair of shoetrees. Shoetrees preserves the shape of the shoes and it prevents them from turning up like clown shoes.
- Wear a belt or suspenders, but never wear both. The belt should match your shoes.
- Remove earrings or other pierced objects from your body.
- Your hair should be well combed and brushed. You may want to get a haircut.
- Refrain from using heavy smelling grease or hair sprays.
- Remove loose facial hairs or five-o-clock shadow from your face.
- Always unbutton your suit jacket when you sit.

Women

- It is strongly recommended that ladies wear a skirted suit. Recommended colors: navy blue, black, dark gray or brown. Refrain from wearing corduroy, plaids, jeans, suede or leather.
- Wear a white, off-white or pastel colored blouse.
- Minimal jewelry (remove piercings from your body other than your ears). Wear one set of conservative earrings.
- Wear minimal makeup and project a natural look.
- Avoid wearing perfume or cologne.
- Refrain from using heavy smelling grease or hair sprays.
- You should wear your hair in a natural color and avoid wearing roots or color streaks.
- Hair should be neatly styled. Individuals with long hair should wear it in a business style look.
- Fingernails should be well manicured and refrain from wearing false fingernails with fancy designs.
- Wear conservative shoes with heels no more than one inch and a half. Do not wear white.
- Shoes should be shined. Refrain from wearing slip-on, open-toe, or open-back shoes with straps.
- Wear conservative type stockings that match your suit. Do not wear fish net or jewel design or light colored stockings.

Chapter X

"The power behind you is greater than the task before you."
- Archbishop Barbara Harris -

JOB SEARCH STRATEGIES

Conducting a job search involves knowing about yourself, developing strategies that will help you target employers and the ability to follow through with your game plan. All too often, many job seekers fall short of landing a job because they failed to develop a game plan. An aggressive approach is essential in conducting a job search and it should include the following tips:

Establish a job objective – It is important for you to develop a clear definition of the job that you are seeking.
Self-assessment – Conduct a self-assessment of your experience, abilities and skills and determine which types of jobs match your talents.
Resume - Devise a resume that highlights your skills and capabilities that are applicable to the job that you are seeking.
Utilize career services contacts - Utilize career services professionals from your school or at the local colleges to assist you in your job search.
Take advantage of your professional network to learn of job leads. Include everyone you know from family, work, school, friends, and associates. (See Chapter XI on networking) <u>Seventy percent (70%) of all jobs obtained in the U.S. are through networking</u>.
Respond to newspaper ads, magazine ads and attend job fairs.
When responding to job openings, always submit a well-written cover letter and resume in a 9 x 12 inch envelope.

Conduct follow-up telephone call a week after you have sent out your cover letter and resume.

Devise a record keeping system to keep track of the employers who you have contacted. (name of employer, address, telephone, contact person, title, name of position, the date that the resume was sent, response information) You may use index cards, a notebook or a computer to record this information.

Research potential employers through various career resource guides such as:

Black Collegian
National Job Bank
The Hidden Job Market
Job Choices – Minority Edition
Equal Opportunity Magazine
Minority Opportunities
Hoovers Business Directory
Job Hunter's Sourcebook
Federal Jobs Digest
Careers & the Disabled

Also, you can extend your job search by utilizing the Internet at such websites as:

Job Web - www.jobweb.com
Career Hunter – www.careerhunter.com
Monster – www.monster.com
Career Builder – www.careerbuilder.com
Super Job Search – www.superjobsearch.com
Job Bank USA – www.jobbankusa.com
USA Jobs (The federal government website) – www.usajobs.opm.gov
America's Job Bank – www.ajb.dni.us
Job Options – ww1.joboptions.com

More important, don't get discouraged if you receive rejection letters. It's part of the process. <u>Remember, the person with the most homeruns usually has the most strikeouts.</u>

Chapter XI

"Life's most persistent and urgent question is what are you doing for others?"

- Rev. Dr. Martin Luther King, Jr. -

NETWORKING: AN ANCIENT TOOL FOR TODAY'S JOB SEEKER

Networking has been the underlying factor in the survival of the human species since the beginning of time. Among African civilizations, networking was the essential element in the construction of the pyramids, the African metal age, and many other successful periods on that large continent.

So what is networking?

Networking is a system for accessing and tapping into information, resources, and support that might not necessarily be available to the general public. Often, these contacts are someone you already know. Today's job seekers can increase their chances of finding a position by using the age-old concept of networking. According to the National Center for Career Strategies, 70% of the jobs in this country are obtained through networking while another 14% are found through advertisements. Evidence shows networking to be a highly productive method in uncovering the hidden job market.

The primary reason for using the network system is to acquire specific information that will give you the edge in the job market. A tip from a colleague or friend could alert you to a potential job opening not yet advertised. Better yet, that same person could be familiar with the specific type of individual that company wishes to employ.

Tapping into your people information base can provide the key to your successful job search. The average person interacts with approximately 20-25 people per day. Networking is maximizing every contact. The success of your job search will depend on your ability to employ all of those resources around you and to use that information to devise a sound game plan.

Sound Network
A sound network game plan includes the following tips:
   Set goals that clearly define the direction you intend to take.
   Assess your skills and capabilities, and focus on positions that match your abilities.
   Utilize career services professionals at your college or university to assist you in your job search. Many of these individuals may have the inside track on current openings, or they may provide you with a contact with a prospective employer.
   Capitalize on your current or past academic faculty network by contacting your professors to learn of job leads. Other key contacts include colleagues at work, school, friends, family, and other associates.
   Attend job and career fairs and talk with employer representatives. Make sure you get their business cards for a familiar inside contact.
   Research potential employers through various resource guides in the career services library.
   Join professional organizations and attend conferences. Many of these professional organizations provide information on job openings for its members and conference participants.

   Evidence shows networking to be a highly productive method in uncovering the hidden job market.
   Set up informational interviews with potential employers.
   Aside from these tips, the success of utilizing the network system in your job search will require you to be steadfast and diligent. It still holds true. Sometimes, it is not as important what you know, but who you know when it comes to landing the job.

Chapter XII

"An obstacle is what you see when you take your eyes off the goal."

- Anonymous -

THE CAREER FAIR: A WINDOW OF OPPORTUNITY

A career fair is an opportunity for you to meet with employer representatives on an informal basis to discuss career information and employment opportunities. It is another form of networking that can help you get your foot in the door of an employer through careful planning. A major part of the planning process for a career fair is developing a list of questions to ask the employer representatives.

SOME QUESTIONS TO ASK EMPLOYER REPRESENTATIVES
1. What characteristics does a successful person have at your organization?
2. Could you describe a typical day?
3. What are the best and worst parts of your job?
4. How important are professional degrees or credentials for entrance and promotion in this field?
5. Is demand for your kind of work increasing, stabilizing, or decreasing?
6. How could you utilize my skills?
7. Are there internship possibilities with your organization?
8. Is there anything I can do to make myself more qualified for this type of work?

SOME QUESTIONS TO ASK YOURSELF
1. Will I be seeking information only?
2. Will I want to generate interviews?
3. Should I dress in business attire?
4. Is my resume ready to distribute?

5. What questions should I ask?
6. Should I bring a pad and pen?
7. Will I need to think about follow-up?
8. Where can I get further information?

Chapter XIII

"There is no greater agony than bearing an untold story inside you."

- Maya Angelou -

SALARY NEGOTIATION

Throughout this book, I have continuously emphasized the importance of developing a plan for each phase of the career planning process. Salary negotiation is another process that involves strategic planning. All too often, job candidates find this process to be troublesome because they don't want to oversell or undersell themselves to employers. Your success in negotiating a salary will be determined by proper planning and research. Listed below are several steps for successful salary negotiation.

Research the salary for the position that you are negotiating for. This information can be obtained from your career services center, the local library, career publications, business and trade journals and the Internet.

After you have conducted your research and retrieved the salary information, assess your skills and abilities to determine a salary range. (Example: "Based on my experience and educational training, I'm looking at a salary range of $30,000 to $40,000.) If you have participated in some form of field experience such as an internship, cooperative education or apprenticeship, include these hands-on activities as experience when constructing a salary range.

Always maintain your poise after the employer presents you with an offer. Don't be quick to respond to the offer. Successful salary negotiations are a result of the candidate's ability to remain cool, calm and collective.

If an employer asked you, what do you really want? Pause for about 25-30 seconds and request the highest amount in your salary range.

If, they don't accept it, you still have room for further negotiations, which will hopefully lead both you and the employer to a common ground.

After you and the employer have agreed on a salary and compensation package, request a copy of the agreement in writing.

If you have offers from more than one employer, review each package plan carefully and determine which plan meets your needs and goals. Example: one employer may offer you a lower salary with a compensation package that includes tuition reimbursement. This package plan may be beneficial to you, if you have plans of obtaining another degree, certification or further training in your field.

Chapter XIV

"A positive attitude is the one characteristic that all successful people have in common."

- Anonymous -

PROFESSIONALISM IN THE WORKPLACE

Professionalism in the workplace is a particular form of business etiquette, which is an important element in achieving success in the workplace. It is the quintessential way professional businessmen and women conduct themselves. Business etiquette relies on tradition, social expectations and behavior standards. Although sound office manners may not be listed in your job description, they definitely play a crucial role in your career. Your career success will depend on your ability to incorporate business etiquette and life-long learning skills into your daily activities.

Life-long learning skills are those skills that have been honed and refined. They are retrievable on demand to negotiate effective outcomes. Employees gain valuable training through many vehicles including employer-training programs. In fact, employers spend over $40 billion dollars annually for employee training. <u>We live in a skill-oriented society</u>. Employees who do not continually seek opportunities inside and outside the workplace to constantly upgrade their skills are expendable. Occupations continue to increase their educational requirements with no end in sight. Employers want individuals who possess an array of transferable skills.

What are transferable skills?
Transferable skills are the set of skills that are transferable from one job to another. They may consist of the following:

Able to analyze information *Managing/Supervising*
Adaptability *Negotiating/Arbitrating*
Budget management *Organizing*
Communication *Personal management*
Computer literate *Problem-solving*
Critical thinking *Processing information*
Editing *Public speaking*
Fluent in another language *Reading*
Group effectiveness *Researching*
Interviewing *Teaching/Instructing*
Leadership *Time management*
Listening *Writing*

Listening and oral communication skills quickly rise to the top as vital skills because these skills encompass most of our daily activities at work. The average person spends 8.4% of communication time writing, 13.3% of reading, 23% speaking and 55% listening. Therefore, communication skills are crucial to success on the job. Furthermore, employers go to great lengths to identify adaptable team members.

Adaptability, personal management, group effectiveness and influence are major factors that attribute in one's personal and professional development. Progressive businesses and organizations want individuals who are flexible and able to keep pace with new developments in technology, changes in the marketplace and new management practices. Employees who are innovative problem-solvers are highly sought after in today's business world and are less likely to be the victim of budget cuts.

Personal management consists of an assortment of skills such as self-esteem, goal-setting and personal/career development. Self-esteem is necessary for employees to take pride in their work and goal setting helps motivate them to achieve stated objectives. It is important for you to learn how to advance within an organization and what opportunities exist outside your present employer.

Group effectiveness is another key element in the success of any organization. In today's marketplace, it is imperative that workers understand and practice teamwork, negotiation, and interpersonal skills. Individuals who learn how to work effectively in groups are the backbone of progressive organizations that build successful businesses and programs. Aside from working effectively in groups, each person must institute their own influence in order to successfully contribute ideas to an organization. It is important to understand the organizational structure and informal networks in order to implement new ideas or complete certain tasks.

Success in the workplace will not be derived from your academic or technical knowledge or experience. It will be a direct result from your ability to utilize proper business etiquette and communicate effectively. Non-verbal communication actions such as handshakes, body language and eye contact are used instinctively to evaluate a person and form a first impression.

Business Do's and Don'ts
- Be careful with your appearance (proper hygiene and wearing the right clothes)
- Be friendly (getting along with your supervisor and co-workers)
- Learn the culture of the organization
- Honor other people's territory
- Learn how to do your job and expand your knowledge
- Communicate and listen
- Don't use regional or slang expressions
- Utilize professional development programs
- Punctuality and attendance
- Keep an open mind
- Follow through with work/projects assignments
- Keep personal information to yourself
- Be positive and supportive
- Don't borrow money

- Try to solve your own problems
- Don't be in a too big a hurry to advance

Good office manners means good business and it also plays a crucial role in your career. If you know what to do, when to do it and how to do it with grace and style, you will have the competitive edge in the workplace. Professionalism in the workplace is understanding the employer's expectations and setting personal goals.

Chapter XV

"It must be borne in mind that the tragedy of life doesn't lie in not reaching your goal. The tragedy lies in having no goal to reach."

- Dr. Benjamin E. Mayes -

PREPARING FOR GRADUATE SCHOOL

Obtaining a graduate degree is another attainable goal that provides a stepping-stone for career success. It can improve your career position economically, enable you to qualify professionally and it provides the gratification that higher learning offers. Therefore, it is imperative for you to understand the importance of choosing the right graduate program. Proper research and guidance are important factors for helping you select the program that fits your needs.

Tips for Applying to Graduate School

Conduct an honest evaluation of yourself and your academic record to determine if graduate school is for you.

It is important for you to conclude that graduate school is part of your career goals. Individuals will sometimes pursue a graduate degree for a number of reasons unrelated to their career goals, including pressure from their parents or a need to keep up with their friends.

It is important that you understand the graduate education and the admission process. Some of the questions that you should ask yourself are:
- Where should I apply?
- What programs am I reasonably competitive for admission?
- What colleges will best serve my interests and capabilities?
- Will I be attending graduate school out of state or locally?
- How will I finance my education?

Explore the various program options and select the programs that are appropriate for your talents (**www.petersons.com**). Also, there are a number of innovative graduate programs that may match your needs and interests.

Make an honest assessment of your academic qualifications. If you are weak in a particular academic area, you should consider taking courses in that field to strengthen it. Also, it is important for you to develop a specialization such as computers, research or language skill that will entice graduate schools to want you.

Find out which graduate school standardized test you need to take (GRE, GMAT, LSAT, MCAT, MAT) and how you can prepare for it.

Complete the admission process to the letter and <u>do not deviate from it</u>. Read the admission application thoroughly before you complete it.

Compose a strong personal statement that markets your strengths and abilities, and have a faculty member or someone professional critique it. The admission essay is designed to give the admissions committee at graduate schools an idea of who you are. When writing an admission essay you should include the following things about yourself:
- Motivation and commitment to a field of study
- Major areas of interest
- Writing ability
- Expectations with regard to the program and career opportunities
- Research or work experience
- Educational background
- Immediate and long-term goals
- Reasons for deciding to pursue graduate education in a specific field at a particular institution
- Leadership qualities

Find out if you qualify for an application fee waiver. It could save you a lot of money. If possible, you may want to visit the school.

Investigate the many ways to finance graduate school.
- Inquire about fellowships, assistantships, scholarships and grants.
- Develop your financial plan for graduate school (tuition cost, books, housing cost, etc.).
- You may need to complete the Graduate and Professional School Financial Aid Service (GAPSFAS) form.

10. If you have questions during this process, don't be afraid to contact your career services center for assistance.

Chapter XVI

"Failure to recognize possibilities is the most dangerous and common mistake one can take."
- Mae Jemison -

FINANCIAL AID

Financing your education through outside sources may consist of grants, loans, work-study or scholarships. A majority of the financial aid programs are derived from the federal government. It is important for you to understand the application process, because it can prevent you from experiencing problems further down the road. To avoid from being scammed by financial aid research services, contact the financial aid office at the school that you plan to attend. Also, you may contact the Federal Student Aid Information Center (1-800-433-3243) or the financial aid office at your local community college for guidance.

- Grants – Grants are for undergraduate students, which do not have to be repaid. The amount of the grant is based on need.
- Loans – Loans consist of borrowed money that must be repaid with interest. Undergraduate and graduate students may be eligible to borrow money through certain loan programs.
- Work-study – Affords students the opportunity to earn while attending school to help finance their education.
- Scholarships – Students must meet specific requirements to qualify for scholarships. When applying for scholarships, it is important for you make sure that you are eligible and that you have completed the application correctly.
- Financial Aid and Scholarship Sites - www.studentaid.ed.gov or www.fastweb.com

Furthermore, a number of colleges conduct workshops or seminars on financial aid, which are generally open to the public.

(Source: U.S. Department of Education - Federal Student Aid Information Center)

Chapter XVII

"We must turn to each other and not on each other."
- Jesse Jackson -

RESOURCES

Obtaining a successful career will require commitment on your part to developing a plan of action that clearly defines your interests, skills, personal traits and values through self-assessment. Charting your career path will require you to include the following steps:

1. Set your career goals and write them down.
2. Develop a plan of action and follow it to the letter. Make a "To Do" list. Remember, plan your work, work your plan.
3. Conduct research on career related and educational information.
4. Build a network of contacts: seek assistance by utilizing professional contacts, such as teachers, career counselors, community leaders for guidance and resources.
5. Align yourself with individuals that have the same aspirations as you. You don't need to be around people with negative attitudes.
6. Don't let any distractions disrupt your plans. Keep your eyes on the prize.

Information is power, therefore it is a necessity for you to arm yourself with the resources needed in guiding you down your career path. Listed below are a number of resources that can be found in your high school guidance office, your local library, and the career services center at your local colleges and vocational schools.

- Encyclopedia of Careers and Vocational Guidance
- Black Collegian

- National Job Bank
- Occupational Outlook Handbook
- The Dictionary of Occupational Titles
- The Hidden Job Market
- Job Choices – Minority Edition
- Equal Opportunity Magazine
- Minority Opportunities
- Hoovers Business Directory
- Job Hunter's Sourcebook
- Federal Jobs Digest
- Careers & the Disabled
- Eight Steps to Helping Black Families Pay for College – The Princeton Review
- The Last Job Search Guide You'll Ever Need – College Recruiter
- Succeed Magazine
- Simplicity Magazine
- Managing Your Career (Published by the Wall Street Journal)
- Career Development Guide Magazine

Chapter XVIII

"Racism is not an excuse to not do the best you can."
- Arthur Ashe -

REFERENCES

- Dictionary of Occupational Titles – U.S. Department of Labor
- Encyclopedia of Careers and Vocational Guidance – J.G. Ferguson Publishing Company
- Equal Opportunity Magazine - Equal Opportunity Publications, Inc.
- Hoover's Handbook of American Business – Hoover's Business Press
- Minority Opportunities: The Directory of Special Programs for Minority Group Members – Elizabeth Oakes (7th Edition)
- Minority Organizations; A National Directory – Elizabeth Oakes (5th Edition)
- The Last Job Search Guide You'll Ever Need – College Recruiter
- The Resume Catalogue: 200 Damn Good Examples – Yana Parker
- 8 Steps to Helping Black Families Pay for College – The Princeton Review
- U.S. Department of Education - Federal Student Aid Information Center
- Peterson's Career Guide to Colleges, 5th Edition

"We're a winner and never let anyone say boy, you can't make it, cause a feeble mind is in your way."
— *Curtis Mayfield* —

SCHOLARSHIPS

1) Bell Labs Fellowships For Under Represented Minorities
   http://www.bell-labs.com/fellowships/CRFP/info.html

2) Student Inventors Scholarships
   http://www.invent.org/collegiate/

3) Student Video Scholarships
   http://www.christophers.org/vidcon2k.html

4) Coca-Cola Two Year College Scholarships
   http://www.coca-colascholars.org/programs.html

5) Holocaust Remembrance Scholarships
   http://holocaust.hklaw.com/

6) Ayn Rand Essay Scholarships
   http://www.aynrand.org/contests/

7) Brand Essay Competition
   http://www.instituteforbrandleadership.org/IBLEssayContest-2002Rules.htm

8) Gates Millennium Scholarships
   http://www.gmsp.org/nominationmaterials/read.dbm? ID=12

9) Xerox Scholarships for Students
   http://www2.xerox.com/go/xrx/about_xerox/about_xerox_detail.jsp

10) Sports Scholarships and Internships
    http://www.ncaa.org/about/scholarships.html

11) National Assoc. of Black Journalists Scholarships (NABJ)
    http://www.nabj.org/html/studentsvcs.html

12) Saul T. Wilson Scholarships (Veterinary)
    http://www.aphis.usda.gov/mb/mrphr/jobs/stw.html

13) Thurgood Marshall Scholarship Fund
    http://www.thurgoodmarshallfund.org/sk_v6.cfm

14) FinAid: The Smart Students Guide to Financial Aid Scholarships
    http://www.finaid.org/

15) Presidential Freedom Scholarships
    http://www.nationalservice.org/scholarships/

16) Microsoft Scholarship Program
    http://www.microsoft.com/college/scholarships/minority.asp

17) Wired Scholar Free Scholarship Search
    http://www.wiredscholar.com/paying/scholarship_search/pay_scholarship_search.jsp

18) Hope Scholarships & Lifetime Credits
    http://www.ed.gov/inits/hope/

19) William Randolph Hearst Endowed Scholarship for Minority Students
    http://www.apsanet.org/PS/grants/aspen3.cfm

20) Multiple List of Minority Scholarships
    http://gehon.ir.miami.edu/financial-assistance/Scholarship/black.html

21) Guaranteed Scholarships
http://www.guaranteed-scholarships.com/

22) Boeing Scholarships
http://www.boeing.com/companyoffices/educationrelations/scholarships

23) Easley National Scholarship Program
http://www.naas.org/senior.htm

24) Maryland Artists Scholarships
http://www.maef.org/

26) Jacki Tuckfield Memorial Graduate Business Scholarship
http://www.jackituckfield.org/

27) Historically Black College & University Scholarships
http://www.iesabroad.org/info/hbcu.htm

28) Actuarial Scholarships for Minority Students
http://www.beanactuary.org/minority/scholarships.htm

29) International Students Scholarships & Aid Help
http://www.iefa.org/

30) College Board Scholarship Search
http://cbweb10p.collegeboard.org/fundfinder/html/fundfind01.html

31) Burger King Scholarship Program
http://www.bkscholars.csfa.org/

32) Siemens Westinghouse Competition
http://www.siemens-foundation.org/

33) GE and LuLac Scholarship Funds
http://www.lulac.org/Programs/Scholar.html

34) CollegeNet 's Scholarship Database
http://mach25.collegenet.com/cgi-bin/M25/index

35) Union Sponsored Scholarships and Aid
http://www.aflcio.org/scholarships/scholar.htm

36) Federal Scholarships & Aid Gateways 25 Scholarship Gateways from Black Excel
http://www.blackexcel.org/25scholarships.htm

37) Scholarship & Financial Aid Help
http://www.blackexcel.org/fin-sch.htm

38) Scholarship Links (Ed Finance Group)
http://www.efg.net/link_scholarship.htm

39) FAFSA On The Web (Your Key Aid Form & Info)
http://www.fafsa.ed.gov/

40) Aid & Resources For Re-Entry Students
http://www.back2college.com/

41) Scholarships and Fellowships
http://www.osc.cuny.edu/sep/links.html

42) Scholarships for Study in Paralegal Studies
http://www.paralegals.org/Choice/2000west.htm

43) HBCU Packard Sit Abroad Scholarships
http://www.sit.edu/studyabroad/packard_nomination.html

44) Scholarship and Fellowship Opportunities
http://ccmi.uchicago.edu/schl1.html

45) INROADS internships
    http://www.inroads.org/

46) ACT-SO Olympics of the Mind
    http://www.naacp.org/programs/actso/actso_index.html

47) Black Alliance for Educational Options Scholarships
    http://www.baeo.org/options/privatelyfinanced.jsp

48) ScienceNet Scholarship Listing
    http://www.sciencenet.emory.edu/undergrad/scholarships.html

49) Graduate Fellowships For Minorities Nationwide
    http://cuinfo.cornell.edu/Student/GRFN/list.phtml?category=MINORITIES

50) Rhodes Scholarships At Oxford
    http://www.rhodesscholar.org/info.html

51) The Roothbert Scholarship Fund
    http://www.roothbertfund.org/schol

"The greatest gift that you have is your mind, because it allows you create and do great things."

www.ingramcontent.com/pod-product-compliance
Lightning Source LLC
Chambersburg PA
CBHW052112070526
44584CB00017B/2452